Beginning

TENNIS

Coach Marc Miller and
the following athletes
were photographed for
this book:
  Ryan Burnet,
  Charissa Coleman,
  Christina Coleman,
  Ryan Ford,
  Neil Kolatkar,
  Molly Purdy,
  Heidi Rovick,
  Charlie Schultz,
  Mary Beth Schultz,
  Philip Woo.

Beginning
TENNIS

Julie Jensen

Adapted from Marc Miller's
Fundamental Tennis

Photographs by Andy King

Lerner Publications Company ● Minneapolis

Library of Congress Cataloging-in-Publication Data

Jensen, Julie, 1957-
    Beginning tennis/by Julie Jensen ; adapted from Marc Miller's Fundamental Tennis ; photographs by Andy King.
        p. cm. — (Beginning sports)
    Includes bibliographical references and index.
    ISBN 0–8225–3500–9
    1. Tennis—Juvenile literature. [1. Tennis.] I. King, Andy, ill.   II. Miller Marc.   Fundamental Tennis.   III. Title. IV. Series.
GV996.5.J46   1994
796.342—dc20   93–48385
                                                      CIP
                                                       AC

Manufactured in the United States of America

1 2 3 4 5 - I/HP - 99 98 97 96 95

Photo Acknowledgments
Photographs are reproduced with the permission of: p. 7, The Bettman Archive; p. 8, (top) The Inter-national Tennis Hall of Fame and Tennis Museum at the Newport Casino, Newport, R.I.; (bottom) The Bettman Archive; p. 9, (top) Sportschrome East/West, Rob Tringali, Jr.; (bottom) Sportschrome East/West, Gilbert Iundt; p. 55, UPI/Bettman.

Contents

Chapter 1

HOW THIS GAME GOT STARTED

Tennis is an action-filled sport. A skilled tennis player must be fast. Quick hands and feet also help. Size and weight aren't important when you play tennis.

To be a good tennis player, you also need a strong and sharp mind. You must focus on what is to be done next. And a good tennis player stays cool and calm under pressure.

Tennis is a great sport to learn and master. You can play it your whole life. Youngsters can begin playing tennis when they are 2 or 3 years old. Adults have been known to play when they were in their nineties.

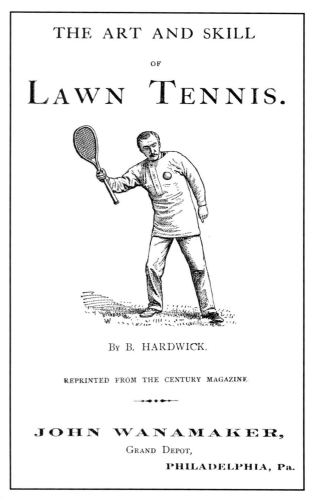

An early tennis handout

Major Walter Clopton Wingfield

The first tennis matches probably were played on stone courts with hard, rough balls. Rubber balls were invented in 1850. That changed the game of tennis forever. In 1873 Major Walter Clopton Wingfield made up the game we call tennis. He lived in England. One year later, Mary Ewing Outerbridge introduced the game to the United States.

Some 33 tennis clubs formed the United States Lawn Tennis Association in 1881. The name of the group was later changed

to the United States Tennis Association (USTA). The USTA has more than half a million members. An estimated 22 million Americans play tennis.

The USTA holds the U.S. Open Tennis Championships each year. The USTA also runs programs for children and adults. Famous tennis players such as John McEnroe, Chris Evert, and Andre Agassi have played in the USTA program.

Chris Evert

Chris Evert was one of the greatest women tennis players ever. Her father, James Evert, was a tennis teacher. He began giving her lessons when she was 6. They would go down to the local park, and he would toss balls to her. At first, Chris missed nearly every ball. But soon she was showing signs of great talent.

Chris played in her first tournament when she was 8. She entered her first professional tournament as a 15-year-old. She played as an amateur because players could not turn pro until they were 18.

Chris's favorite playing surface was clay. She won more than 100 tennis matches in a row on clay courts. Her two-handed backhand was the key to her game.

Few athletes have ever dominated a sport as Chris did before she retired in 1989. But she also was a model of sportsmanship. She was kind and considerate on and off the court. Players, coaches, and fans all over the world admire her.

Andre Agassi at the French Open

Chapter 2

BASICS

The main idea of tennis is to hit the ball over the net and inside the **court**. If you can do this one more time than your opponent does, you will win.

Singles is tennis that is played by two players, one against one. When four players are playing two-against-two, the game is called **doubles**. The **doubles alleys** add 4½ feet to each side of the court for playing doubles.

Across the middle of the court is a net. The most important lines on the court are the **singles sidelines**, the **doubles sidelines**, the **service line**, and the **baseline**.

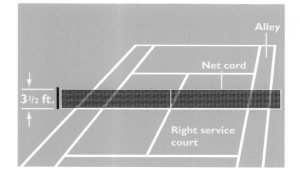

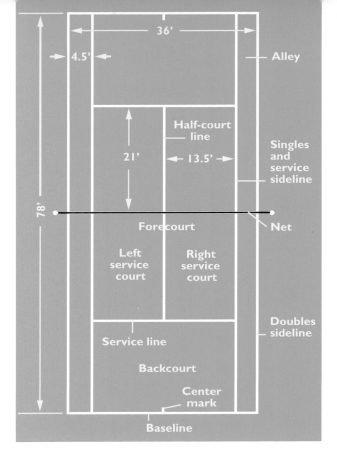

Balls

A tennis ball's hollow rubber frame is covered with a nylon-wool fabric.

The Court

Tennis was called "lawn tennis" at first because most matches were played on grass courts. Today, tennis is played on concrete, asphalt, clay (dirt), grass, and even on indoor carpet. The weather and what's available where the courts are built determine which surface is used. For example, India has very little clay. So some courts are made of cow poop that is rolled, flattened, and hardened. This makes a great tennis court but smells a little when it rains!

Styles of Play

*The surface of the court determines how players play tennis. Surfaces like clay are rough. They slow the ball down. These courts are called **slow courts**. To win on slow courts, a player must be steady and fit. Points on slow surfaces often last a long time.*

*Surfaces like grass are slick. The ball bounces low and fast. Courts with these surfaces are called **fast courts**. On fast courts, players need to hit the ball hard and deep.*

The Racket

Rackets come in many shapes and sizes. Most rackets are built with layers of materials. These layers give the racket strength and power. They also keep the racket light so the player can swing it rapidly. Racket handles come in different sizes. Every player should be able to find a racket he or she can hold comfortably. The hitting surface of a racket is a tightly strung net of nylon or other synthetic strings.

The Clothes

A tennis player wears loose-fitting clothes—like shorts, a T-shirt, and tennis shoes—that allow quick movement.

Shoes are the most important part of a tennis player's clothing. Tennis shoes need to have good treads so that players do not slip and fall during play. They should fit well to prevent blisters. Shoes also should support a player's ankles and knees. Running shoes are not good for playing tennis because they are not built for the quick side-to-side movements tennis players make.

Strings

Most brand-new rackets do not have strings. Strings are made from many materials. Most strings today are synthetic gut string made from nylon.

Ask a professional or teacher to help you pick out the correct racket. Then, have a professional racket stringer string your racket. A professional will know the best type of string for you and your racket. Having a racket strung usually costs between $15 and $30.

Socks

Many tennis players wear two pairs of socks to prevent blisters. Thick socks made of cotton are best for tennis.

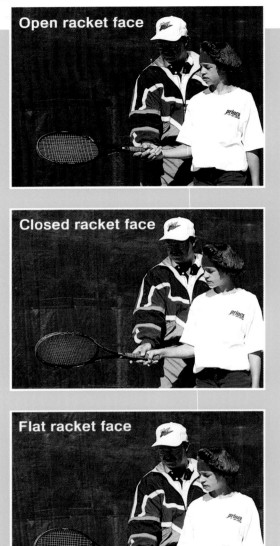

Open racket face

Closed racket face

Flat racket face

Racket Faces

The racket face is open if the strings of the racket face upward. When the strings face downward, the racket face is closed. The racket face is flat when the strings face straight ahead. Most strokes are hit with a flat racket face.

The Strokes

The basic moves that tennis players make are called **strokes.** Four strokes are the building blocks of a tennis game: the **serve,** the two **ground strokes** (forehand and **backhand**), and the **volley.**

The serve is the only stroke that you begin by yourself. All other strokes are used after your opponent hits the ball.

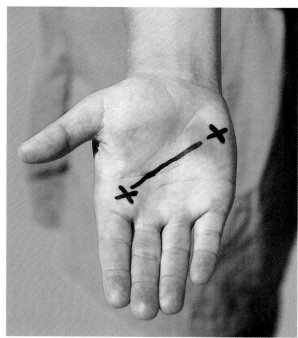

Grips and the Grip Line

The way a player holds his or her racket is called a **grip**. Look at the line drawn on Ryan's hand from the base of his index finger to the pad of his hand. This line shows the grip line. The grip line is used to find the correct grip for each stroke.

All racket handles have eight sides. Imagine that the end of a racket is a clock. The top edge of the racket is at the 12:00 position, and the next edge to the right is between 1:00 and 2:00. The next two edges are at 3:00 and between 4:00 and 5:00. The fifth edge is at 6:00.

If Ryan puts his grip line at 12:00, he has an Eastern Backhand grip. When the grip line is between 1:00 and 2:00, the grip is a Continental grip. At 3:00, the grip is an Eastern Forehand grip. When the grip line is be-tween 4:00 and 5:00, the grip is called Semi-Western. A grip that is all the way below the handle at 6:00 is called a Western grip. To find the correct grips for the strokes, match the grip line on your hand to the correct side of the racket (clock).

The Serve

The goal of a serve is to hit the ball into the service box diagonally across the net from you. The ball can't hit the net.

Most players use a Continental grip to serve. An Eastern Forehand grip works fine too. The service motion is like a throwing motion. If you can throw a ball, you can serve. The two basic parts to the serve are the toss and the swing.

Watch a professional match on TV to find a model for your perfect serve. The serve is one long, fluid motion. Try to imagine a good, long motion before beginning to serve.

The Stance

This is the **stance,** or beginning position, for the serve. Ryan is sideways to the target with his left shoulder pointing toward the net. He is not facing his target on the other side of the court in this position. Ryan is right-handed. If he were left-handed, his right shoulder would point toward the net. Ryan's arms are loose and relaxed and hanging down by his hips.

The Toss

The toss is the most important part of the serve. If your toss is the same every time and you have a strong throwing motion, then you will have a strong serve. The toss should go up to the highest point that you are able to reach with your racket.

Let go of the ball only when your tossing arm is stretched as high as it can go. Then the ball should go only about 1 foot out of your hand before it is hit. Think of it this way: If someone asked you to toss 100 balls into a bucket that was only a foot away from you, how many balls would you make in the bucket? Probably 100! What if you had to toss the balls in a bucket that was 5 feet away? If you release the ball from waist high when serving, you have to toss the ball 4 to 5 feet. You'll probably miss some of the tosses.

Look again at Ryan's serve. He has released the ball from the highest point with his arm stretched toward the sky. The ball also is a little in front and a little to the right (for a right-handed player) of his front foot.

The V Position

The racket must be ready to hit the ball right after the toss is released. Both arms come up together in a **V position**.

Ryan's left hand has released the toss. His racket hand is up and ready to swing at the ball. This is the classic position for the serve. In fact, most tennis trophies have a figure in this position at the top of the trophy!

Over the Net

The back-scratch position allows the server to hit up into the ball on the serve. You would have to be 13½ feet tall to be able to hit down on the ball and still get it over the net. No one is 13½ feet tall. We have to hit up on the ball to get it over the net.

The Rhythm of the Serve

The key to pulling the serve together is rhythm. Let's call the ball toss and the V position #1. The back-scratch position is #2. The point of contact is #3. If we were counting out these numbers during a good serve we would say, "..1.......2.3." The first part of the motion is slow and easy (..1.....). That makes the ball toss accurate and consistent. Once the ball is released, go as fast as possible (..2.3.). The faster the motion, the harder the ball will be hit. Remember, racket speed gives the ball zip.

The Back-Scratch Position

In the **back-scratch position**, the racket moves from the V position down the back. It looks like the racket is being used as a back-scratcher. This happens when the server rotates forward toward the target. The server must let the racket "fall" down his or her back as the server's body is turning forward.

The Point of Contact

The **point of contact** is the place where the ball and the racket meet. Ideally, the point of contact is on the strings in the center of the racket. This point should be as high as you can reach with your racket and out in front of the baseline a little bit.

Ryan is reaching for the ball at the point of contact. His eyes are still focused on the ball.

The Finish

After the ball is hit, the **finish** for the serve should be long and smooth. The racket hand should finish so your thumb ends up on your left pocket (right pocket for a lefty). Ryan's hand has finished across his body near his left pocket. Most servers will finish inside the baseline about 2 or 3 feet. If you have served correctly, your momentum will carry you in the direction of your serve. If your momentum carries you sideways, your ball toss was off to the side one way or the other.

The Recovery

Even though your serve is completed, you are not finished. After hitting the serve, you need to **recover** your court position. If you stand 2 or 3 feet inside the baseline after your serve, you will not be in position for your opponent's return. After hitting the serve, move back to about 1 foot behind the baseline and near the middle of the court. Then you will be ready to hit your next shot.

Ground Strokes

Ground strokes are shots that are hit after the ball bounces on your side of the court. Right-handed players hit a forehand on their right side. Right-handers reach across their bodies to hit a backhand. Left-handers hit a forehand on their left side. Lefties reach across to hit a backhand on the right side.

Low-to-high

Forehands and backhands are hit with a low-to-high motion. At the start of the swing, the racket is below the ball (low). By the end of the swing, the racket finishes above the ball (high). With this motion and a flat racket face, the ball is lifted over the net but lands inside the baseline.

The Ready Position

To get in the **ready position**, like Neil, bend your knees comfortably. Balance your weight slightly on the balls of your feet. Relax your grip. Hold your racket about waist high.

The Forehand

The Grip

The Eastern Forehand grip is used for the forehand. The grip line is on the racket handle at the 3:00 position. (Turn to page 15 to review the racket edges.)

The Preparation

Think of hitting the forehand with your whole body. Turn your body sideways as your racket goes back. Neil's racket is pointing to the back fence and his eyes are focused on the ball. Neil's legs are slightly bent.

The Point of Contact

As the stroke begins, Neil's racket head drops below the ball. He'll be able to stroke the ball with a low-to-high motion. The racket moves forward toward the ball because Neil's hips and shoulders have rotated forward toward the net.

The ball and racket meet at a position that is even with his front foot. The racket face is flat and Neil's eyes are focused on the ball. As the racket moves forward to the ball, Neil's weight also shifts to his front foot.

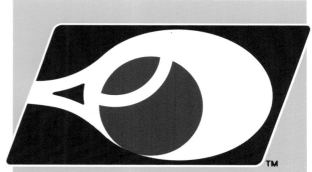

A League of Your Own

One of the best ways to start playing tennis is to join the USTA's National Junior Tennis League (NJTL). The League was founded in 1968 by Arthur Ashe. The goal of the NJTL is to help young athletes learn teamwork, cooperation, and competition by playing tennis.

There are more than 500 NJTL chapters across the United States. Write to the USTA for the NJTL chapter nearest you. The USTA address is on page 62.

The Finish

As Neil strokes the ball, he extends his racket out toward the target. After hitting, Neil's racket goes up and over his left shoulder. Neil can look directly over his hitting elbow and see his target on the other side.

The Recovery

Neil finishes balanced and controlled. He can quickly recover his position and get ready for the next shot. Neil recovers by using shuffling steps, moving his feet side to side. Don't cross your feet when you recover your court position. It is difficult to change directions with your feet crossed. If you shuffle, you can change directions and run for the next shot with ease.

Hitting Ground Strokes

Ground strokes can be hit from anywhere on the court, but they are often hit near the baseline. Ground strokes are usually hit **crosscourt** (from one corner of the court diagonally across to another corner) because the court is longer that way.

The Backhand

You can hit a backhand with one hand or with both hands. Many players use one hand for a quicker shot and a longer reach. Others use both hands for more power and better control.

Heidi gets ready for this shot by turning her body and pulling back her racket. Her racket points to the back fence and her shoulders are sideways to the net.

Two-Handed Backhand

The Grip

The grip for the two-handed backhand is actually two forehand grips, one with each hand. For a right-hander, the right hand is on the bottom. For a left-hander, the left hand is on the bottom.

The Point of Contact

After this great preparation, Heidi rotates her hips and shoulders toward the net. This pulls her racket forward so that she hits the ball when it is even with her front foot. Heidi's racket face is flat. Her eyes are focused on the ball.

The Finish

Heidi's legs are straightening as she finishes. This shows how she uses her entire body and not just her arms to hit the ball. Her racket finishes high and above her right shoulder. She can look over her left elbow and see her target on the opponent's court. She is also balanced in this position so that her recovery will be quick.

The Recovery

Heidi does not stand and admire her backhand. Instead, Heidi shuffles back near the middle of the court. She stays on her toes and positions herself about 1 foot behind the baseline.

The point of contact

The finish

One-Handed Backhand

The Grip

Most players hitting a one-handed backhand use an Eastern Backhand grip. To form this grip, place your grip line on the 12:00 edge of the racket handle.

The Preparation

As his opponent hits the ball, Charlie rotates his shoulders back. He uses his left hand to help him change his grip to a backhand grip. His shoulders are sideways to the net.

The Point of Contact

Charlie steps toward the ball. His arms begin to spread so that the racket goes forward to meet the ball. The point of contact on a one-handed backhand is 1 to 1½ feet in front of the front foot. Charlie's left hand is moving toward the back fence, away from the racket hand.

The Finish

Charlie's arms have spread apart. His body is still sideways to the net at the finish. His racket finishes high above his head.

The Volley

Court Position

A volley is hit before the ball bounces. It is an attacking stroke used to finish the point. A volley can be hit from the forehand or backhand sides. It generally is hit from halfway between the net and the service line.

The Grip

Use the same grip for a volley as you used for the ground strokes. More advanced players often use a Continental grip, which allows them to use the same grip for both forehands and backhands. Volleying tends to be quick because the play is so close to the net.

The Preparation

When volleying, keep your racket in front of your body with your racket head up. Your first move when volleying is to point the racket face at the ball.

The Point of Contact

The point of contact for the volley is in front of and away from your body. The volley doesn't require a swing. The power comes from stepping into the ball with the racket in front. Neil is stepping into the ball as he gets ready to hit the forehand volley. On many volleys, you must take several steps just to get to the ball. Mary is moving several steps to hit this backhand volley. Both Neil and Mary are watching the ball as they hit.

The Finish

There is no finish on the volley. For accurate and solid volleys, the racket face should point to the target after the ball leaves the racket. After hitting the volley, recover your court position so that you can hit the next ball.

SINGLES

Charlie stands behind the baseline, looking across the net at his opponent. He calls out the score, "40-30," knowing that with one more point he'll win the match. He tosses the ball gently into the air. With blazing speed, he hits his serve. The ball skids off of the service line to Phil's left side. Phil lunges and hits a solid forehand deep into Charlie's court.

Charlie runs to the ball and lifts it deep into Phil's court. Phil didn't expect such a deep cross-court return. He runs full speed to catch up to the ball, but he is too late. Charlie wins! Both players meet at the net to shake hands after their exciting match. This is the game of singles—two players matching their skills against each other.

Playing by the Rules

You have to be honest when you play tennis. In most tennis matches, players act as their own umpires and referees. Players decide whether a ball lands inside or outside of the lines on their side of the court. All balls that are not clearly outside the line must be called "in" and played.

A USTA Code of Conduct card explains some of the rules of tennis. It describes the behavior that is expected of all players. These cards are available from the USTA. See page 62 for the address of the USTA office.

Tennis players have to keep track of the score themselves. Both players have to watch the ball carefully. A ball is inbounds when it lands inside or touches the singles line. A ball is out of bounds when it lands clearly outside of the singles lines. Players do not call "in" when balls are in. They do call "out" when the balls are out.

Other rules must be followed when playing tennis. The ball is allowed to bounce only once on each side of the court. If the ball bounces twice on your side, stop playing and give the point to your opponent. If you touch the net at any time during the point, you lose the point. If you reach over the net to hit the ball, you lose the point.

Sometimes a ball will hit the top of the net and still land in the correct service box. On a serve, this is called a **let**. The server gets to serve again for a replay. Sometimes it happens during play. If the ball lands inside the court, the opponent must run forward and hit it to the other side. A let can also be called by either player when anything rolls or blows onto the court during play.

Scoring

Before you and another player can start a game, you must decide who will serve first. You also must choose which side of the court you will play on first. Players switch sides after each game.

A player scores a point when the ball bounces more than once on the opponent's side. If one player hits the ball into the net or outside the court, the other player gets a point.

Both players have zero points when a game begins. Zero is called **love** in tennis. The points in a game of tennis are: love, 15, 30, 40, and game. The server calls out the score before every serve. The server's score is called first.

How Long Is a Tennis Match?

A tennis player never knows for sure how long he or she will be playing. The length of a basketball or football game is set by a clock. But a tennis match is played until it's over. Most tennis matches last between 1-2 hours. Some matches are over in 25-30 minutes.

Two women once played a match that lasted 6 hours and 22 minutes. Vicky Nelson and Jean Hepner were playing in a tournament in Richmond, Virginia, in October 1985.

Vicky Nelson won the match in two sets, 6-4, 7-6. One point lasted for 643 hits. Each player hit the ball 322 times before that point ended!

A player wins a **game** by winning at least four points and having at least two more points than the other player. The first person to win six games wins a **set**. But the person must win at least two games more than his or her opponent. The first player to win two sets wins the **match**. Most matches are best-of-three sets.

If the score of a game is tied, 40-40, the score is called **deuce**. A player must win two points in a row to win a deuce game. When the server wins one point, the score is **ad-in**. When the server's opponent wins one point after deuce, the score is **ad-out**.

If both players win six games in a set, a **tie-breaker** is played. Players play 12 points in a tie-breaker. The first player to score 7 points wins, if he or she has won at least two more than his or her opponent.

Wheelchair Tennis

Tennis can be played by athletes of different physical abilities. Wheelchair athletes hit the same shots as able-bodied players do, but the rules for wheelchair tennis are slightly different.

When serving, a wheelchair player must keep the rear wheels of the chair behind the baseline until the ball is hit. The wheelchair player cannot come out of his or her seat to hit any shot.

But a wheelchair player can let the ball bounce twice. The first bounce must be inside the court. The second bounce can be anywhere. Wheelchair players move to where they can hit the ball on the second bounce. The ball is moving slower then, and is in a more comfortable spot for them to hit it. This means that positioning the wheelchair is very important.

The National Foundation of Wheelchair Tennis has books and videotapes that show the right wheelchair moves. The foundation also can give you the names and phone numbers of wheelchair tennis programs in your area. Contact the foundation through the USTA. The USTA address is on page 62. Get those wheels rolling!

The Server

The server begins every point in a tennis match. The server must serve from the right side of the court to start a game.

Molly is standing behind the baseline. She is between the **center mark** and the singles sideline. Molly must get the ball in the **service box** diagonally across the net from her. Molly has two chances to get a serve in. If she misses on both tries, she loses a point. That is called a **double fault**. Molly's serve will be called out if she crosses the baseline before the ball is hit. That is called a **foot fault**. If Molly's opponent can't return the serve, Molly has served an **ace**.

Molly switches to the other side of the center mark after each point is played and serves to the other service box.

The Returner

The returner can stand any-where on his or her side of the court. If Molly misses the serve, Heidi yells loudly, "Fault." If the serve lands in, Heidi tries to hit the ball across the net.

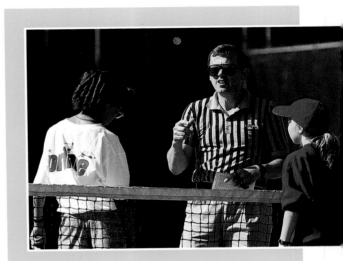

Umpires

Umpires may be at some of your matches, especially at tournaments. Umpires help make sure the rules of tennis are followed. Treat all umpires with respect. They are there to help you have a fun, fair game.

There are three kinds of tennis umpires. Some umpires are roving umpires. These umpires keep an eye on many courts at one time and help players with problems.

Other umpires are called line umpires. You have seen these umpires in tennis matches on TV. Line umpires sit along the various lines on a tennis court. They call the balls in or out on that line.

A chair umpire sits at the net in a chair. The chair umpire is in charge of the whole tennis court. He or she keeps score. The chair umpire also corrects any line calls that are incor-rect during a match.

Singles Strategy

Most points are scored because of errors, not great shots. Many mistakes end up in the net. Use the low-to-high motion in your stroke. Hit the ball solidly on the strings. Then if you miss, you will miss deep or wide. It's better to miss your shots either deep or wide. Your opponent might try to hit them anyway.

First, learn to control your shots. Next, find your opponent's weak spots. Does he or she make more errors on the forehand or backhand side? Try to hit all of your balls toward your opponent's weaker side.

Then, think about defense. Sometimes you will have to scramble to get to your opponent's shots. When you are

scrambling, hit softly. Remember, good players do not make many mistakes. Hit the ball well inside all of the lines.

After every match, shake your opponent's hand. Whether you win or lose, say something good about your opponent's play. Sometimes this is hard to do, especially if you lose a close match. Remember, you cannot become a better player unless you play against better players. Learn something from every match that you play, whether you win or lose.

Finally, thank your mom or dad or brother or sister for bringing you to play or practice. Those who help you need to hear "Thanks" every day!

Chapter 4

DOUBLES

Doubles is a team game. Two players play together, move together, think together, and win together.

The rules for doubles play are the same as those for singles. However, players can use the doubles alleys. This means that the court is 36 feet wide. Although the court is wider, the service box stays the same size.

Serving Team

Either player on the serving team can serve first. This person serves for the entire game. Once a game is finished, the other team serves. Teammates take turns serving games for the rest of the set. The server stands between the center mark and the doubles sideline. The server's partner stands in the middle of the service box that is not in front of the server.

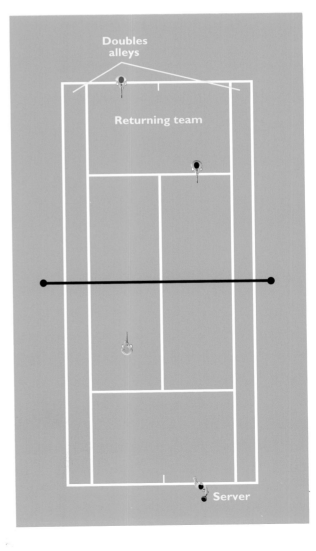

Returning Team

One player plays on each side of the court. Once a set begins, the players must start on their side for the rest of that set. When the set is over, the players may change sides.

Phil and Mary are preparing to return a serve. Phil is at the baseline. Mary is at the service line. This is the one-up and one-back position. The two teammates have clear roles. Mary is the up person. She is the attacker. She will try to hit as many volleys as possible. Phil, the back person, is like a center fielder in baseball. He hits any balls Mary can't reach. The back person hits most of the balls back.

Doubles Strategy

It is almost impossible to hit winning points from the baseline. Most points are won close to the net. This means that the back person should run to the net as soon in the point as he or she can. A doubles team is in its strongest position when both players are at the net.

When Charlie hits the ball down the alley to Phil, Phil will hit the ball between Charlie and Molly. Look at the hole between Charlie and Molly. There is no way that they can cover all of this space. There is much less space between two players at the net.

The **lob** is a high shot that is hit over your opponent's head. We'll explain just how to hit the lob in the last chapter. The lob keeps the ball away from the net person, who will score most of the points. Charlie is lobbing over Mary's head and running to the net. Phil is turning to chase the lob and Mary is switching sides to cover for Phil. This is how teammates cover the lob.

Charlie lobs over Mary's head.

Phil runs back after the lob...

...as Mary moves to cover his side.

Phil prepares to return the lob.

Another strategy is to hit the ball down the middle between the two players. That is a team's weakest spot when both players are at the net. Charlie is hitting the ball between Phil and Mary. Neither can cover the shot.

It is very important that the two players talk to each other during points. If you feel that you can hit the ball, call loudly, "Mine." This tells your partner that you'll get the ball. He or she can get ready for the next shot.

Teammates also should talk between points. Try to figure out what your opponents are thinking. Discover your opponents' weak spots.

Find a partner you enjoy and play some doubles. Doubles is a game that everyone should try!

Chapter 5

PRACTICE, PRACTICE

Now you have learned a little bit about tennis. But how can you improve? What should you practice?

Pick one or two skills to work on first. Practice those strokes until you feel you are good at them. Then work on another stroke. You will develop a solid game this way.

Warm up each time that you go out to play or practice tennis. Jog, jump rope, or do any other activity that will make you sweat. Then you can begin stretching. Warming up and stretching will help you avoid hurting your muscles.

49

Practice Progression

Here's a drill to get you started. Mary stands next to Heidi. She drops the ball at Heidi's side. Heidi hits the ball at a target on the other side of the net. Heidi is able to think about her stroke because the action is slower than in a match. She hits 10 or 15 balls over the net. Then Heidi drops balls for Mary.

Practice Success

Your practice time can be a blast! Smacking balls over the net is fun. So is sweating a little while you and your partner get better.

Hitting balls back and forth with your partner is difficult when you are a beginner. After one or two hits, you will have to pick up the balls.

Instead, try building on each skill you master. Take your time. Learn the basic skills well. Build a strong base with your strokes. You will have the most fun when you are hitting the balls over the net and into the court.

Tossing to Each Other

Next, Mary backs up about 10 feet. She is off to the side so that she will not get hit by Heidi's forehand shots. Mary tosses balls, so that Heidi can stroke them over the net. Then Mary tosses balls so that Heidi has to run before she hits the ball.

Feeding Each Other

Once each player can do the tossing drill, the players can hit by themselves. Heidi drops a ball and hits it to Mary. Mary catches the ball and tosses it back to Heidi. After both girls can do this successfully, Heidi hits the ball to Mary so that Mary can hit it back to her without catching it first.

This practice, called feeding each other, helps the players learn how to react quickly to the ball that the opponent is hitting.

Rallying

Heidi and Mary can feed each other. Now they are ready to hit the ball back and forth over the net without the ball stopping. This is called **rallying**. Heidi and Mary begin to rally standing at the service lines instead of at the baselines. This keeps the pace of the balls a little slower. When they can hit 10 or 15 balls over the net without a miss, they move back to the baselines to rally using the whole court.

> **Fitness Test**
>
> *The USTA Fitness Protocol tests show an athlete how he or she compares with other tennis players in strength, endurance, and speed. If you want to learn more about the test, contact your local USTA office for a copy. Or write to the USTA. The address is on page 62.*

Practicing with a Wall

How can you practice by yourself? A wall or garage door is the perfect practice partner. Drop the ball and hit it to a target. Then catch the ball as it bounces off the wall.

Can you do this five times in a row without missing? If you can, drop the ball and hit the wall again. But as the ball bounces back to you, hit it back to the wall. You will have to get ready after each hit or the ball will sail back to you before you can react. Try to keep the ball going for 5 to 10 hits in a row. Don't worry about hitting the ball hard. Hitting the ball with good form is more important.

Fitness

A tennis player has to be able to hit the ball while moving, and be able to change direction quickly. A tennis player needs to hit the ball hard and at the target. To do all these things, a tennis player has to be in good shape.

Conditioning

There are two types of conditioning that can be done by a player. **Aerobic (air-OH-bik) conditioning** is long-distance exercising. It builds up a player's endurance and stamina. Jogging, bicycling, and swimming are aerobic conditioning.

With **anaerobic (an-air-OH-bik) conditioning,** a player's strength and power improves. Sprinting, hopping, and jumping are anaerobic conditioning.

Strength Training

You can become stronger by resistance training. During resistance training, you add a weight, or some other form of resistance, to your exercise. This kind of training overworks certain muscles. When a muscle is overworked, it rebuilds itself to be stronger than it was before. A coach should watch you when you are training.

RAZZLE DAZZLE

The more you practice and play, the better you'll be at playing tennis. And the better you become, the more you'll want to play at the net. At the net, you can win points by hitting balls your opponent can't reach. Your opponent won't even know what whizzed past his or her ear—and it will be your point!

As you improve, you can add some trickier shots to your game. One of these is the **lob**.

Bjorn Borg

Bjorn (bah-YORN) Borg was born in Sweden. Bjorn's father was one of the best table tennis (Ping-Pong) players in Sweden.

When Bjorn was 9, his father gave him a tennis racket. Bjorn began to play tennis. He hit balls with topspin. That is the way table tennis players hit Ping-Pong balls. Balls hit with topspin drop sharply. Bjorn hit forehands with a Western grip. He hit his backhands with a two-handed grip. By doing this, he was able to hit all his shots with a lot of topspin.

Bjorn won the French Open Championship when he was 17. When he turned 19, he won the first of his five Wimbledon titles. He retired in 1983.

56

The Lob

Molly is hitting a lob. Molly's racket is well below the ball as she swings at it. Her racket face is open. The lob is different from a ground stroke. Molly hits the ball on the bottom. This makes the ball sail high into the air. Molly ends this stroke with her arm high above her head as her racket extends to her target.

The target for the lob is important. A lob follows the shape of

a rainbow. The highest point, or peak, in a lob's "rainbow" is directly over the net. If the peak of the rainbow is over Molly's side, the lob will be short. Her opponent will have an easy shot. If the peak of the rainbow is over her opponent's side of the court, the ball will land outside the court.

Hit a lob when your opponent is at the net. Make him or her run back to the baseline. Then you can go to the net.

The Overhead

Phil is at the net. Neil is hitting a lob over Phil's head. He wants Phil to run back to the baseline and let the ball bounce before hitting it. But Phil is going to hit the ball while it is in the air above his head. This is called an **overhead**.

Being in the right position for an overhead is important. Phil's racket hand is behind his head in the back-scratch position. His other hand is up in the air.

The point of contact for the overhead is almost the same as for the serve. The ball should be a little bit in front of Phil's body. He will hit it when it is as high as he can reach with his racket.

The drop shot is almost a baby lob. It lands just over the net. Mary is preparing for this shot. She is watching the ball. Mary's racket face is slightly open, as for a lob. Her swing is very short because she wants to hit the ball just over the net. But notice how her finish ends up high again. Most people trying to hit the ball short wind up hitting the ball into the net. This is because they end the shot with a short, low finish.

Hit the drop shot from near the service line. From there, a soft little shot can just sneak over the net. Hitting a drop shot from near the baseline is difficult. The ball needs to travel too far in the air before it crosses the net. Remember, all you are trying to do is bring your opponent to the net.

The Drop Shot

The **drop shot** forces the other player to run toward the net for short balls. Let's say that you are playing against someone who is beating you on too many points from the baseline. But your opponent's volleys are not very good. You want to force your opponent to hit volleys. The drop shot is the answer.

Being a Winner

The action and excitement of tennis attract millions of people. They have fun on tennis courts —at Wimbledon or their local park. Now you can too!

TENNIS TALK

ace: A serve that an opponent doesn't return.

ad-in: The score when the server wins a point to break a 40-40 tie in a game.

ad-out: The score when the server's opponent wins a point to break a 40-40 score in a game.

aerobic conditioning: Developing endurance with exercises that increase your heart rate and breathing rate, such as jogging and swimming.

anaerobic conditioning: Developing strength with exercises that increase your muscle strength, such as weight lifting.

back-scratch position: The point during a serve when the racket head is at the middle of your back.

backhand: A ground stroke hit by reaching across your body so that the back of your hand swings out at the ball; can be done with one or two hands.

baseline: The line parallel to the net that marks the end of the court.

center mark: A short mark in the center of the baseline that defines the service area.

court: Flat rectangular area on which tennis is played; 78 feet long; 27 feet wide for playing singles, 36 feet wide for doubles; divided by a 3-foot high net.

crosscourt: From one corner of the court to the corner diagonally across.

deuce: Tie score of 40 points each.

double fault: Both serving attempts by a player land outside the service box or in the net.

doubles alleys: Areas 4½ feet wide on each side of the court used when playing doubles.

doubles sidelines: Lines on the court marking the doubles alleys.

doubles: Tennis played by four players, two against two.

drop shot: A short shot that lands just over the net.

fast courts: Courts with surfaces, such as grass, that are slick.

finish: A player's position after a stroke has been completed.

foot fault: A server steps on or over the baseline before the ball is hit.

forehand: A ground stroke hit on the same side of the body as the hand holding the racket, so that the palm of the hand swings toward the ball.

game: A series of four or more points, with one player scoring at least two more points than an opponent.

grip: The way a player holds a racket in his or her hand.

ground stroke: Any stroke used after the ball has bounced on your side of the court.

let: A ball that hits the top of the net and lands on the other side of the court; also the term used to call for a replay if another ball or object is on the court during play.

lob: A high, arching shot.

love: Scoring term for zero.

match: Three sets; the first player to win two sets wins the match. (Male professional tennis players play best-of-five-set matches.)

overhead: Hard swing from above your head at an opponent's shot, much as for a serve, but hit during a point.

point of contact: Where the ball and the racket meet.

racket: A lightweight bat with a long handle and netting stretched across an open oval frame.

rally: Players hitting the ball back and forth over the net without the ball stopping.

ready position: The stance your body is in while waiting to hit a shot; knees bent, weight slightly on the balls of your feet, your racket loose and about waist high.

recover: To regain your balance and position after you hit a shot.

serve: The stroke used to put the ball in play at the start of each point in a game.

service box: The rectangle marked off on the court by the net, the service lines, and the sideline, that is diagonally across the net from the server.

service line: The line 21 feet from the net that defines the service box.

set: Six or more games, with one player winning at least two games more than his or her opponent.

singles sidelines: The lines that define the sides of the court for singles.

singles: Tennis played by two players, one against one.

slow courts: Courts with rough surfaces that slow down the ball and give it a higher bounce.

stance: A player's beginning position for a stroke.

stroke: Movement of the racket designed to hit the ball over the net and in the court.

tie-breaker: A 12-point play-off to decide the winner of a set after both players have won six games. One player must win at least seven points and at least two more than his or her opponent.

V position: The point during a serve when your racket is raised above your head and your other arm has just released the ball for the toss.

volley: Any shot that is used to hit the ball before it bounces.

FURTHER READING

Braden, Vic and Bill Bruns. *Vic Braden's Quick Fixes*. Boston, Massachusetts: Little Brown, 1988.

Gallwey, W. Timothy. *The Inner Game of Tennis*. New York: Random House, Inc., 1974.

Klotz, Donald D. *Tennis — Keep it Simple*. Dubuque, Iowa: William C. Brown Publishers, 1989.

Lappin, Greg. *Tennis Doubles*. Edina, Minnesota: KC Books Company, 1985.

Lee, Simon. *Play the Game Tennis*. Great Britain: Ward Lock Limited, 1988.

Lloyd, David. *Fit for the Game Tennis*. Great Britain: Ward Lock Limited, 1991.

Loehr, James E. *The Mental Game*. New York: S. Greene Press, 1990.

Scott, Eugen L. *Bjorn Borg, My Life and My Game*. New York: Simon & Schuster, 1980.

Smith, Jay H. *Chris Evert*. Mankato, Minnesota: Creative Educational Society, Inc., 1975.

FOR MORE INFORMATION

Association of Tennis Professionals (ATP)
611 Ryan Plaza Drive
Suite 620
Arlington, TX 76011

International Tennis Federation (ITF)
Church Road
Wimbledon, London, England SW19 5TF

The National Collegiate Athletic Association (NCAA)
6201 College Boulevard
Overland Park, KS 66211-2422

United States Professional Tennis Association (USPTA)
One USPTA Centre
3535 Briarpark Drive
Houston, TX 77042

United States Professional Tennis Registry (USPTR)
PO Box 4739
Hilton Head, SC 29938

United States Tennis Association (USTA)
70 West Red Oak Lane
White Plains, NY 10604-3602

INDEX